Domestic Abuse Safety Planning with Young Children is accompanied by a number of printable online materials, designed to ensure this resource best supports your professional needs

Go to https://resourcecentre.routledge.com/speechmark and click on the cover of this book

Answer the question prompt using your copy of the book to gain access to the online content.

Domestic Abuse Safety Planning with Young Children

This guidebook is an essential companion to the *Pilgrim's Bumpy Flight* story and is designed to be read by professionals to ensure the effective and safe use of the storybook.

Pilgrims Bumpy Flight has been created to help young children aged 5–7 experiencing domestic abuse, to explore the concepts of physical and emotional safety. Safety planning with a child offers a way to help them vocalise their feelings and understand what to do when something does not feel right. The professional guide will help supporting adults facilitate safety planning that is experienced as emphatically curious, safe and where the child's opinion matters. It provides up-to-date information on domestic abuse, childhood trauma, practice tips and how to complete a safety plan with a young child using the storybook as the key vessel of communication and exploration.

Key features include:

- Accessible information about domestic abuse and coercive control based on the latest research.

- Guidance around direct work and safety planning with young children.

- Practical activities building off Pilgrim's story, including printable material.

- Things to consider and ways to use the storybook to facilitate a conversation with a child, as well as page-by-page helpers notes on the narrative.

- A comprehensive list of helplines and organisations in place to support adult victims/survivors of domestic abuse.

Used alongside the storybook, this professional guide is a crucial tool for the early years sector, education staff and those working in children's services, including safeguarding officers, family support workers, social workers and children's Independent Domestic Abuse Advisors/Advocates (IDVAs). Both books should be used in tandem with agency policy, procedure and guidance.

Catherine Lawler is a qualified specialist children's counsellor, trauma practitioner and childhood survivor of domestic abuse and coercive control. She has extensive experience working with children, young people, adult survivors and families as well as developing and facilitating training on the issues of domestic abuse and coercive control.

Nicky Armstrong, B.A.(Hons) Theatre Design, M.A. Slade School of Fine Arts, has illustrated 30 books which have been translated and published in 7 countries. She has achieved major commissions in both mural and fine art painting.

Domestic Abuse Safety Planning with Young Children

A Professional Guide

CATHERINE LAWLER
ILLUSTRATED BY NICKY ARMSTRONG

Routledge
Taylor & Francis Group

LONDON AND NEW YORK

Designed cover image: Nicky Armstrong

First published 2024
by Routledge
4 Park Square, Milton Park, Abingdon, Oxon OX14 4RN

and by Routledge
605 Third Avenue, New York, NY 10158

Routledge is an imprint of the Taylor & Francis Group, an informa business

British Library Cataloguing-in-Publication Data
A catalogue record for this book is available from the British Library

ISBN: 978-1-032-35800-0 (pbk)
ISBN: 978-1-003-32867-4 (ebk)

DOI: 10.4324/9781003328674

Typeset in AntitledBook
by Deanta Global Publishing Services, Chennai, India

Access the Support Material: https://resourcecentre.routledge.com/speechmark

This book is dedicated to my brother. He is a kind, caring, thoughtful and respectful gentleman. Love you little bro.

Contents

1. Before you use this book

This book focuses on safety planning with children and is for practitioners with a good awareness of domestic abuse and coercive control who will be undertaking safety planning work.

However, in reality, the book's main use with young children will most likely be when they come to our attention after a disclosure or notification of physical violence.

Statistically domestic abuse and coercively controlling behaviours are perpetrated by men with most victims being women. Domestic abuse is one of the most common forms of violence against women and includes physical, sexual and emotional abuse and controlling behaviours by an intimate partner. Domestic abuse occurs in all settings and among all socioeconomic, religious and cultural groups.

However, it is important to acknowledge that domestic abuse occurs in lesbian, bisexual, gay and transgender relationships and in heterosexual relationships where a female may be the perpetrator.

This book aims to be accessible to all children from all families where safety planning is required, and as such the characters in it are non-gendered.

The experience of being read to can often feel nurturing for a child. I hope Pilgrim's story will help children with similar experiences feel less alone and enable them to safely explore strategies they may be able to use when frightening things happen at home.

Before reading the book with a child it is important to read it to yourself. Notice the tone of your own voice and any changes in it as you read the different pages. Does it get quieter, louder, stutter, stick on any particular words or make you reluctant to turn the page?

Do you notice any change in your breathing? Both changes could indicate you are becoming a bit unregulated and moving towards the edge of your window of tolerance. If this was to happen while you are reading the book to the child, the child would notice and may become unregulated in response to your response rather than the content of the book. This is not to suggest you should read the book in a monotone but to make sure you are aware of how your own presentation influences how the message is received.

It is also important to think about the age and language skills of the child you are thinking of reading the book to. Think about what you know about their past or current experiences, who, if anyone, might be annoyed with them or put at risk by the child chatting about the content of the book and what is happening at home.

DOI: 10.4324/9781003328674-1

Keep in mind that safety planning strategies that may work for one child might not work for another. Knowledge of a child's current circumstances, their roles and attachments within their family, and any consequences to them your advice around safety planning may have needs to be addressed and acknowledged.

2. Leaving and post-separation abuse

One of the most frequent questions thought or asked is 'Why don't they just leave?' This question assumes that leaving will end the violence and control and whilst this may be the case for some it is not a true reflection for the majority.

Domestic abuse and coercive control do not necessarily stop when partners separate. In fact, violence and abuse can escalate when the relationship ends (Campbell et al., 2002).

Unlike crimes committed by a stranger, domestic abuse by its very nature has many personal connections. Perpetrators will often exploit these connections as a continuation of their abuse and control. Whether these connections be children, property, finances or family members.

Many victims/survivors are subjected to persistent post-separation violence/coercive control over significant periods of time. Children can be used as a way to gain access to and harass the mother (Beeble et al., 2007).

Katz's (2020, p. 24) research on coercive control-based domestic abuse and its impacts on mothers and children can provide important insights into how children can experience post-separation abuse and coercive control.

> Many domestically violent/abusive fathers often continue to be permitted contact with children; and some children continue to be harmed by their father's/father figure's use of coercive control after their mother's separation from him. These can be some of the most dangerous parents. Yet fewer than 1% of family court cases end up with no contact orders.

Beware the incident-led response model

The nature of domestic abuse is such that families appear to encounter one serious crisis after another. The "incident-led response" is usually driven by "blue-light" crises. However, it is important to remember there may not be a police notification for coercive control which does not include physical violence.

The incident-led response can result in short-term intervention being employed to tackle the immediate risk at the expense of the longer-term outcome. Short-term crisis management can make it difficult for professionals to see the bigger picture and to acknowledge domestic abuse as a continuum of behaviour including the impact of coercive control.

DOI: 10.4324/9781003328674-2

Children experience domestic abuse and coercive control with all their senses. They hear it, feel it, see it, smell it and experience the aftermath and reverberations of it. Children will consciously read a perpetrator's mood in anticipation of possible responses and actively manage themselves in relation to this. Considering this, it is important that safety planning is not viewed as a one-off crisis response activity with a child but a trauma-responsive continuous intervention.

3. Cast of characters

Pilgrim

Pilgrim represents a young child whose home environment is one of domestic abuse. Pilgrim's story portrays the typical feelings a young child may experience when living with domestic abuse and centres around introducing the concept of safety planning.

Jet

Jet represents a victim/survivor parent of domestic abuse who acknowledges Pilgrim's distress and introduces the concept of safety planning.

DOI: 10.4324/9781003328674-3

Jumbo

Jumbo is the perpetrator parent of domestic abuse, whose behaviour causes Pilgrim and Jet anxiety and distress.

4. Page-by-page helpers notes

Page 1. Introduces Pilgrim to the reader. Pilgrim represents a young child who is enjoying learning and trying out new skills.

Page 2. Represents Pilgrim experiencing enjoyment at school, school is fun where new learning and skills are practised.

Page 3. Illustrates Pilgrim experiencing good routines and structure at home, where bedtime and the need for rest and relaxation are important. These routines are initiated by Jet, Jet is the victim/survivor parent.

Page 4. Illustrates Pilgrim having fun with friends.

Page 5. Introduces Jumbo, the perpetrator parent.

Page 6. Jumbo's behaviour is scary to Pilgrim, creating anxiety and worry. This behaviour curtails Pilgrim's natural drive to experience fun and learning at school.

Page 7. Illustrates Jet's empathic connection to Pilgrim. Jet acknowledges that home can feel like a scary place when Jumbo gets mad. In simple and understandable language Jets explains the fight-flight response to Pilgrim.

Page 8. Illustrates Pilgrim's Fight-Flight response activating. This page creates the opportunity for the supportive adult to explain this in more detail and to normalise the response with the child.

Page 9. Jet begins to introduce the concept of safety planning and a support circle to Pilgrim.

Page 10. Shows the supportive and loving relationship between Pilgrim and Jet.

DOI: 10.4324/9781003328674-4

5. Toxic stress

There are three known responses to stress: positive, tolerable and toxic.

Positive stress response is a normal and essential part of healthy development, characterised by brief increases in heart rate and mild elevations in hormone levels. Some situations that might trigger a positive stress response are the first day at school or a visit to the doctor.

Tolerable stress response activates the body's alert systems to a greater degree because of more severe, longer-lasting difficulties, such as the loss of a loved one, a natural disaster or a frightening experience. If the activation is time-limited and buffered by relationships with adults who help the child adapt, a child will recover from what might otherwise be damaging effects.

Toxic stress response can occur when a child experiences strong, frequent and/or prolonged adversity – such as physical or emotional abuse, chronic neglect, caregiver substance abuse or mental illness, exposure to domestic abuse, without adequate adult support. This kind of prolonged activation of the stress response systems can disrupt the development of brain architecture.

All children will experience positive and tolerable stress with positive and tolerable results. The term toxic stress, developed at the Harvard Centre and used by the 70/30 campaigning charity to replace the word trauma, describes the physical impact on the body and the emotional brain when both are overloaded. Experiencing prolonged activation of the stress response system in the absence of protective relationships has a negative effect on the brain and the body (Felitti & Anda, 1998).

The fight-flight-freeze response

Our brain and body are programmed to alert us to dangerous situations, Fight-Flight-Freeze responses describe how our ancestors had to literally fight for their lives or flee to survive physical danger. The **Fight** response is your body's way of facing any perceived threat aggressively. **Flight** means your body urges you to run from danger. **Freeze** is your body's inability to move or act against a threat. These responses are referenced in Pilgrim's story.

In a frightening situation your body may experience the following:

Blood pressure rises.

Heart rate goes up.

DOI: 10.4324/9781003328674-5

Muscles tense.

Hairs stand up on the back of your neck or arms.

Stomach turns over/flips.

Sweating/becoming instantly hot.

Feeling ice cold and clammy.

These reactions are caused by the stress hormones – adrenaline, noradrenalin and cortisol – pushing glucose around the body and filling up its energy tank.

In situations such as domestic abuse these stress responses may be on a continual loop as the need to detect danger is ever present, resulting in the body being required to be in a constant state of readiness.

Pilgrim's story can facilitate a conversation with a child regarding stress responses and what to do when these are experienced.

6. Childhood trauma

Trauma can be described as a powerful response to distressing events or series of events. Complex or chronic trauma is often seen when a person experiences traumatic events over an extended period. Children experiencing domestic abuse and coercive control are at risk of experiencing complex trauma as domestic abuse and coercive control are rarely one-off events, they are a pattern and continuum of behaviour whose impact is accumulative and devastating.

Perpetrators often rationalise their conduct, looking at their world in extremely idiosyncratic ways driven by their own needs without regard to the rights and needs of others. Within this context victims/survivors will experience a range of complex, terrifying and confusing behaviours.

These self-affirming and self-seeking behaviours from perpetrators can have numerous detrimental impacts on victims/survivors: They can keep victims/survivors emotionally invested in their relationships with the perpetrator, provide false hope that "things are better now" or "it's not that bad" and undermine their ability to recognise that the perpetrator is an abusive person (Katz et al., 2020).

Swanson et al. (2014) noted that children living with domestic abuse act as "Miniature radar devices" constantly striving to "predict the unpredictable". Learning to manage what they do and do not say, who they speak to, and how they speak, is a clear strategy that children use in coping with domestic abuse daily.

Fear

Domestic abuse and coercive control are fear conditioned. Perpetrators can easily navigate between being kind and terrifying, thus enabling them to take control of relationships and individuals within a family. This results in children interpreting and re-interpreting their experiences and relationships.

Unlike generalised fear, chronic fear builds incrementally via experience. It is often about trying to predict and avoid harm. Children living with chronic fear will learn to be on high alert and in survival mode all the time. Their experiences, emotions and thoughts have a direct impact on their body as well as their mind.

We all have fears in our childhood: "monsters under the bed", "ghosts", "the dark"; however, children who experience and perceive the world as a dangerous and threatening place are likely to experience prolonged activation of the body stress response system. Stress overloads and specifically overloads of cortisol can damage brain cells in the brain that support learning.

Children living in highly controlled and violent environments find home can be a stressful, unpredictable and frightening place. Many children feel they need to always be on guard in anticipation of something

DOI: 10.4324/9781003328674-6

fear-full happening. This is likely to include pre-occupation not just with their own safety but also with their parent's, sibling's and pet's safety.

The fear may be especially acute when a perpetrator behaves unpredictably by "changing the rules": reacting negatively to situations about which they were previously calm (Monckton-Smith, 2020).

Even though there are commonalities, all individuals' experiences of trauma will be unique to them. Symptoms of childhood trauma may include:

- Irritation and anger.

- Difficulties with self-regulation and managing emotions.

- Nightmares and distressing dreams.

- Difficulty with concentration.

- Sleep difficulties.

- Exaggerated stress responses.

Traumatised children can present as angry, unpredictable, depressed or despondent. "What looks like anger and resentment to those around them, is profound fear and terror radiating throughout their minds and bodies" (Forbes & Post, 2009, p. 76).

Children may perceive the simplest of interactions as threatening, using fight-flight-freeze responses as a coping mechanism. It is important to keep in mind that these reactions are entirely normal for anyone confronted with terrifying situations.

According to Van der Kolk (2014) if an organism is stuck in survival mode its energies are focused on fighting off unseen enemies, and as a result our closest bonds are threatened along with our abilities to imagine, plan, learn and pay attention to other people's needs.

Three factors have been identified as important in how a child responds to trauma and how much harm is caused:

1. The amount and duration of the stress response.
2. How often the stress response has been activated in the child's past.
3. The quality of the child's relationship with the caregivers (Carpenter & Stacks, 2009).

Trusting relationships with supportive adults are of prime importance to children experiencing trauma. It may take a long time for a child to feel secure enough to trust an adult with information that has been a longstanding secret or source of embarrassment or shame. Often, a relationship will need to be built up gradually. However, some children will take the initiative and turn to a trusted adult out of the blue. It is important to listen and be available during such times.

When thinking about the daily lived experience of a traumatised child the A-B-C model may be helpful to support practitioners identify triggers. Following on from this, they may make appropriate adjustments to support the child and avoid similar triggers.

Antecedents

What triggered the outburst/behaviour?

What has happened at home?

Has there been a police notification?

What was the context (day, time, activity, subject)?

What was happening before?

Behaviour

- Describe exactly what happened i.e., the child's response.

Consequences

- What do staff do next?

- How did the child respond?

- What could be helpful or done differently?

7. A child's place within the family

When we think of family life, we would hope to conjure an image of a unit in which all members feel respected, safe and valued. Sadly, for many children this is not the case. Domestic abuse and coercive control can rob a child of their sense of safety, sense of self and sense of value.

In England and Wales 2020/2021 the police made 245,000 referrals to Children's Social Care for domestic abuse. It is estimated that one in five children will experience domestic abuse every year, but that likely underestimates the extent as it counts only those situations that come to the attention of formal agencies, such as those in health, children's social care, the police or schools.

Previously characterised as "witnesses" which implies a passive role, not including hearing, being part of or seeing the aftermath of domestic abuse, we now talk about a child's lived experience/children subjected to domestic abuse/coercice control. Children are often engaged in interpreting, predicting what is happening at home and worrying about themselves and others. They can be abused and/or weaponised by the perpetrator as part of the abuse continuum towards the victim/survivor parent. The term domestic abuse does not necessarily depict the extremity of behaviours and brutalisation that children may experience.

Children may be directly involved by the perpetrator in coercive control activities, including isolation, blackmailing, monitoring activities and stalking, and can be used in other ways by abusers to minimise, legitimise and justify violent behaviour (Johnson, 2008; Stark, 2007).

In Harnes' (2011) research, children and young people describe a catalogue of fathers' cruel and emotionally abusive behaviour towards them, such as destroying schoolwork, school reports and toys, harming pets, not allowing children out of the house/friends to visit the house or to phone, not allowing them to speak to their mothers.

Some fathers are shown to deliberately emotionally abuse children and young people, insulting them and humiliating them in a similar way to their mothers.

Potential impacts on the victim survivor parent

The tactics that perpetrators use to control their victims can result in them living in constant states of fear and disorientation. Victims/survivors will often lose trust and connection with others and with themselves.

DOI: 10.4324/9781003328674-7

They may experience

Confusion

Perpetrators create situations of uncertainty to keep their victims out of kilter – often described as walking on eggshells. Victims/survivors often second-guess themselves and struggle to make decisions. Their main concern is fear of the consequences from the perpetrator for any decisions or choices they make for themselves and their children.

Self-doubt

Perpetrators will often attempt to convince their victim that their actions are coming from a place of love and concern, therefore legitimising their behaviour. This tactic can create doubt in the victim/survivor's mind about the intention of the abuse and make it difficult to challenge.

Blame and shame

Perpetrators often blame their victim for provoking them into violent/abusive behaviours, absolving themselves of any responsibility and suggesting the victim/survivor created and deserved the abuse.

Guilt

Feelings of guilt in victims/survivors can come from multiple sources. Imposed feelings of guilt may come from the perpetrator and from family, friends and services whose expectation is that the victim/survivor should leave. Feelings of guilt can cause victims/survivors to shut down, leaving them more susceptible to the abuse and control they already experience.

Anxiety

Victims/survivors may be plagued by worry about the perpetrator's responses relating to current and future situations, resulting in them experiencing crippling anxiety.

Depression

The cumulative tactics perpetrated by an abuser often result in the victim/survivor experiencing incapacitating depression. Feelings of hopelessness and despair can leave people vulnerable to further abuse and dependency on their abuser.

Lack of joy

All or some of the above can significantly impact the opportunity and expression of happiness joy and relaxation.

Family roles

Having individual roles within families are natural and common to family systems. Family roles shape how we interact with each other and can have positive and negative aspects to them. Domestic abuse and coercive control permeate the family and for some create distortions in relationships and attachments within the family unit.

Below are some of the roles that children experiencing /subjected to domestic abuse and coercive control may have imposed on them, or they may adopt as coping strategies.

The caretaker
A child may act in a caretaking role to the victim/survivor parent/siblings. This may include helping in the household, acting to keep the victim/survivor parent and siblings safe during attacks and comforting them afterwards.

Victim/survivors confidant
A child who may be privy to the adult victim/survivor's feelings, concerns and plans. Collaborative safety planning is ideal in this case.

Perpetrator's confidant
A child who is treated differently by the perpetrator and most likely told justifications for the abuse. The child may be asked to report back on the adult victim/survivor and be rewarded for doing so, for example receiving privileges or the absence of harsh treatment.

Perpetrator's assistant
A child who is co-opted or forced to assist in the abuse of the victim/survivor parent.

The interpreter
A child who attempts to mediate and de-escalate situations. It is not uncommon for children to attempt to divert or de-escalate behaviours within their home as a way of interrupting the development of a perceived abusive encounter. A child may try to prevent violence and control by actively addressing issues perceived as triggers.

The problem child
A child who is identified as the cause of the family problems, blamed for tension or whose behaviour is used to justify violence and control.

Examining possible roles assigned to or adopted by children even if they no longer live with the perpetrator may enable us to understand how a child has interpreted and coped with domestic abuse and coercive control and how this experience may continue to impact the child and their relationships with others.

Domestic abuse and coercive control by their very nature can lead to feelings of powerless and result in the victim/survivor parent feeling overwhelmed with simple day-to-day tasks. They may have limited opportunity to spend time with or talk to their child about what is happening at home and rectify any distorted narratives coming from the perpetrator. It is not uncommon for a victim/survivor parent to be unsure of how to talk to their child about the abuse or feel that by not talking to their child they are protecting them. Safety planning may provide the first safe and structured opportunity for a parent and child to have time together to explore what is happening at home.

8. Children's agency, direct work and safety planning

Children's agency

The term agency describes a child's capacity to proactively act, influence and interpret the shape of their childhood. Children have a right to have their lived experiences understood and to have their voices heard. They also have a right to adequate support and resources to enables them to contribute to matters which affect them (Convention on the Rights of the Child, United Nations, 1989).

A child's voice is an expression of their agency, conveying their intentions, hopes, grievances and expectations (Pufall & Unsworth, 2004).

It is well documented that domestic abuse and coercive control can have catastrophic short- and long-term impacts on children. However, many children experiencing domestic abuse and coercive control have the capacity to understand abusive and controlling dynamics within their families, actively resist them and create their own coping strategies.

Direct work

The immediate purpose of communication is to get in touch with children's real selves, what they are feeling about themselves and their lives. Our presence, attitudes, behaviours and tone of voice are all communicating something to the child.

We are powerful agents in the lives of children, and we need to convey our concern for them as individuals so that they can have the opportunity to perceive us as supportive agents. Often this can be done simply by our remembering something about the last time we saw the child or something that child has said. Something the child has said will have far more significance to him or her than anything we might have said. He or she will feel known, special. Children desperately need us to listen to them. Inside each child is a story that needs to be told, a story that no one has yet had time to listen to. It is through expressing themselves that children get to know themselves and sort out their confusions and develop their own self-image (Claire Winnicott, 1977).

DOI: 10.4324/9781003328674-8

Focusing on the needs and experiences of children is crucial. A failure to adequately understand and respond to children's experiences means there is a high risk that the emotional and psychological impact of domestic abuse will go unaddressed. Children who experience domestic abuse fundamentally want to feel safe, listened to and understood.

Unfamiliar situations such as direct work may cause a heightened state of awareness/arousal for children and their sympathetic nervous system, (the fight- flight-freeze response) may be turned on. This is useful when in danger but within a situation where direct work is being facilitated it can impair a child's ability to listen, engage and take in or retain information. Ensuring we consciously do our best to enable a child to feel relaxed and safe during direct work will hopefully enable them to help turn down the sympathetic nervous system and allow the parasympathetic nervous system to turn on, helping with rapport building, where trust and a sense of safety can be developed.

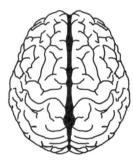

Parasympatheic Nervous System (PNS)		**Sympathetic Nervous System (SNS)**
Constrict pupils		**Dilate** pupils
Stimulate saliva		**Inhibit** salivation
Slow heartbeat		**Increase** heartbeat
Constrict airways		**Relax** airways
Stimulate activity of Stomach		**Inhibit** activity of Stomach
Stimulate gallbladder		**Inhibit** gallbladder

Some children may be reluctant to engage in structured direct work for a variety of reasons, for example they may:

- Fear punishment or repercussions if they do.

- Have a lack of trust in adults.

- Experience guilt and shame.

- Find the work frightening.

Direct work- things to consider

The venue reflective activity – if you are a child experiencing domestic abuse:

- How would the venue need to look and feel to make it safe and comfortable?

- How would you like to be welcomed into the venue?

- How would you like to be greeted by the practitioner?

- What would the practitioner say? how would they introduce themselves and their role? The purpose of the work?

- How do they know about what's happening in your home?

- How do they explain what's going to happen next?

- How do they make it clear that you can choose what happens in the session/sessions?

A pleasant consistent space for a confidential session is vital each time you meet. Children need to feel comfortable if they are to begin to talk about their worries. Predictable places and routines reduce anxiety.

Welcoming the child and rapport building

Introduce yourself and your role. Try and initiate conversations by talking about something neutral, for example "Hi nice to see you, I like your trainers" emphasising you are here to listen as well as to talk to the child about feeling safe and unsafe at home. Ideally this work should take place over several sessions. Thought needs to be given with regard to a child taking any work home or keeping it in a folder in the safe keeping with the helping adult.

Asking the child unrelated questions at this stage may be helpful, i.e., all about me getting to know you curiosity questions. Reassure them you will work at their pace, and they will not be forced to engage if they do not want to. It is important that your work does not replicate the feelings of disempowerment that some children may carry due to the perpetrator's behaviour.

Talk with, not to or at, for example

I'm here to listen, what you tell me is important, but it's also important to me that you feel okay when we are together. So, if you don't want to talk right now that's okay. Any questions asked must be experienced as empathically curious. This empathic response aims to regulate the child's arousal. When introducing activities you may want to think about how sentences are phrased, ie "This book looks interesting, shall we see if it is?" or "This activity looks interesting, shall we see if it is?"

Be creative

Direct work should not be a one-off session it should be planned and have meaning. Of equal importance is the notion of rapport building and free play. Structured work can sometimes feel scary to children. Having a toolkit with lots of fun free-play activities is essential before any structured safety planning work takes place. Part of this toolkit should include basic mindfulness practices, aiming to foster mind-body connections, positive coping skills and feeling present and connected in the moment.

Through using mindfulness practices a traumatised child can better learn about the connection between their minds and bodies and access different ways to assist their minds and bodies calming down (Black & Fernando 2014).

Be open and honest

According to Sheppard (2010), "Children are usually scared or confused about why you want to see them. Misconceptions need to be cleared before any trust can be built. It is good to ask children why they think you want to talk to them". Confidentiality will need to be addressed.

Acknowledge concern

Making empathic statements verbally and non-verbally, active listening, reflection and clarification demonstrate respect and concern.

Think about endings as well as beginnings

We need to consider endings to sessions and endings of direct work. Familiar tools or activities can be used to support positive session endings and provide a sense of structure and familiarity. For example, a jar filled with objects that represent the number of sessions you have together can be used, with one object being removed after each session, providing the child with a visual countdown of your time together.

Safety planning

What is a domestic abuse safety plan?

A safety plan is a way of communicating with a child about their lived experience. It is an activity that aims to explore possible core safety planning points that can be used when there is violence or fear within the home. Safety planning is a key activity within child safeguarding and ideally should be done collaboratively with the victim/survivor parent. Knowledge of the victim/survivor's safety plan and safety strategies already used is essential. They will know what will and what will not work in their family and for their children.

Domestic abuse is not static and by its very nature the perpetrator will aim to keep people in states of uncertainty. For these reasons safety plans need to be reviewed and revisited. It is of particular importance that the plans of adults and children are reviewed when a victim/survivor is considering leaving or has a left, remembering that the risk increases significantly during these times.

All safety plans should be unique to each child, knowledge of the child's role and relationships within the family are imperative. The plan should reflect the reality of the child's age and stage of development as well as their current circumstances.

Things to consider when developing a safety plan with a child:

1. Age.
2. Developmental functioning.
3. Physical health status/disability.
4. Attachment to the victim/survivor parent.
5. Attachment to the perpetrating parent.
6. Age appropriateness of any strategies suggested, i.e., is the child capable/competent to carry them out.

Using Pilgrim's story to safety plan

Introducing the concept of safety

When describing what a safety plan is and why we may need one it can be helpful to have generalised discussions about safety, i.e., road safety, fire drills. Clarity your belief that it's not a child's responsibility to keep people safe at home, and they are not responsible or to blame for things that adults do. Explain that safety planning is an activity to help a child to think about what may help them when they feel scared/unsafe within their family.

Using Pilgrim's story to create a helpers map

Helpers maps are a visual means for a child to show who is in their network (be that family, friends, neighbours, school staff support worker, pets) and what sort of relationships they have with them. Developing a helpers map with a child can identify relationships that are strong and resilient. Helpers maps are not static as family relationships and circumstances change, therefore they should be revisited and dated as should all work.

Activity 1 – Shall we fill in a helpers map just for Pilgrim? The cut-out characters can be coloured in by the child and placed on Pilgrim's helpers map (Appendix 1 and 2)

The following questions may help with this.

I wonder what Pilgrim needs to be ready to learn to fly?

(Pilgrim needs help with learning to fly, might need petrol in their tank, sleep, food, encouragement)

I wonder who might help with this?

(Might be parents, family, school)

Pilgrim has learned how to do loop the loops. Who might have helped Pilgrim learn this?

(Might be parents, family, teachers, friends)

It feels like Pilgrim has fun when doing loop the loops and zooming around. I'm curious, who does pilgrim have fun with?

(Might be friends)

Sometimes Pilgrim feels wobbly and doesn't want to do loop the loops, the loops feel small.

I'm curious who might be able to help when Pilgrim is feeling wobbly?

(Might be parent, family, teacher, siblings, social workers, support worker)

Well, it seems like lots of people love and/or care for Pilgrim.

(Parents, friends, teachers, family)

Pilgrim's amazing people is an adaptation of a helpers map. Ask the child to draw who might be the best person to help Pilgrim get from A to B (Appendix 3)

Activity 2 – Shall we make a helpers map just for you? (Appendix 4)

Who do you want to go on your helpers map?

Direct the child to draw a picture of themselves in the middle, then draw who else they want on their helpers map (don't forget pets, pets can provide us with unconditional love, a focal point to the day and cuddles)

Ask the child to tell you about the people on their helpers map.

This activity can also be adapted later in direct work to explain the roles of professionals involved in a child's life. Using third person narrative refer to Pilgrim's story, i.e., I wonder if a police plane may have come to Pilgrim's house **(Appendix 5)**.

Alternative helpers map questions for a child

When working with a child, at the top of the age range for this book, these questions might encourage them to reflect on their own situation.

- Can you tell me who is in your family?

- Who are you closest to in your family? Tell me about them.

- Who else are you close to in your family? Tell me about them.

- Who are you not close to in your family? Tell me about them.

- Is there someone you can go to/ talk to about what happens/ happened at home?

- Who would you like on your helpers map?

Using Pilgrim's story to explore feelings
Use Pilgrim's story to illustrate how children living with domestic abuse and coercive control often feel afraid, which is a normal response. These feelings may be felt as wobbles in the tummy, feeling hot or cold, heart thumping in the chest. Ask the child how they think Pilgrim might be feeling when Jumbo gets mad **(Appendix 6)**.

If appropriate, then ask a child if they have ever felt any of these feelings and explore on a blank body map. Reassure the child these are all normal responses as happens in Pilgrims' story **(Appendix 7)**.

Using Pilgrim's story – going to a safe place

Use Pilgrim's story to explore a safe space. A safe space is away from where the violence, shouting or scary behaviour is happening. Ask the child where a safe space for Pilgrim might be. Then ask the child to draw/build which place they may consider the safest in their home "what room feels safest for you"? **(Appendix 8)**

It is important that children hear the message that their priority should be to stay safe and that this is okay. They are not letting anyone down, they are doing the right thing. It will be helpful if the victim/survivor parent can reiterate this.

Being in a physically safe space does not mean a child will feel psychologically safe. Ask the child what Pilgrim could do when in the safe space. Introduce techniques like slow breathing, drawing and scribbling, cuddling a doll or teddy. Then ask what they may do when in their safe space.

Phoning for help/helpers

For some children it can be helpful to show them how to phone 999 (or equivalent outside the UK) and what they may say when the call handler answers. For example

- My name is ....

- I need the police.

- ... is hurting my mummy/daddy.

- I live at ....

It can also be helpful to introduce a script if a child was to phone ChildLine (or any equivalent helpline outside the UK).

Closing safety planning activity/work

Reiterate it is normal for children to feel frightened when scary things are happening at home.

Clarify where a child's safe space is.

Refer to the child's helpers map to reinforce that there are people who care about the child.

Use familiar tools or activities, i.e., mindfulness to introduce possible calming techniques.

9. Safety planning tips for adults in abusive households

It is important to come from the starting point that a victim/survivor is the expert in their own experience and will be employing safety strategies on a regular basis. Good practice is to enable them to articulate and explore these. Safety plans need to be personalised to the individual and created in conjunction with them. You will find a variety of information and templates for adult safety plans, including the misuse of technology to monitor victims by perpetrators on the website and resource section.

Suggestions when facilitating a discussion regarding safety planning: This is not an exhaustive list.

Explaining the fight-flight-freeze response can be helpful.

What has the victim/survivor done before that has been helpful?

How has this been helpful?

What has the victim/survivor done before that has not been helpful?

How has this not been helpful?

Phone 999 or equivalent outside the UK in an emergency.

Who is in the victim/survivors' support circle (Appendix 9).

Could these people offer accommodation, loan money, be a safe contact?

Do they have a code word or image that their support circle would recognise as an

alert to an emergency?

What will those people do when they receive the code word or image?

Is their phone always charged up in case they need to make emergency calls?

Do they have credit on their phone, or a secret phone to use in emergencies?

Have they planned their escape route from the house? Do they have a set of spare

keys and a bag so they can grab and go?

If they drive and have access to their own vehicle can this be parked where there is

light, if possible, can they reverse into parking spaces not behind closed gates?

DOI: 10.4324/9781003328674-9

Can they check petrol, oil and water to avoid breakdown?

If going out of the house is permitted, are they aware of initiatives such as ask ANI (see websites and resources)?

Are they aware of Silent Solutions, The Bright Sky and the Holly Guard app (see websites and resources)?

Advise not to use alcohol/substances during periods of escalation as these may affect someone's ability to remain alert.

During incidents attempt to stay away from rooms that may pose more risk, i.e., kitchens, garages, bathrooms.

Has a safety plan been devised with the child/children?

Have they been provided with information regarding packing a survival kit for themselves and their child/children (see "women's aid" in websites and resources)?

And finally, have you acknowledged how hard the victim/survivor is working to keep themselves and their children safe?

10. Relationship rights

Recovery rights

Acknowledging you are a victim/survivor of domestic abuse/coercive control can be difficult. If appropriate and at the right time the following can be explored with the victim/survivor parent. When undertaking any work, it should be experienced as empathically supportive, not blaming or shaming. Many victims/survivors, whether they are still in the abusive relationship or have left, will continue to experience symptoms of trauma, use their established coping strategies and may find it hard to think positively about themselves.

I have the right to:

Be my own person.

Have my own opinion.

Trust my opinion.

Change my mind/opinion.

Say NO without feeling fear or guilt.

Make mistakes.

Have time to myself to do things I enjoy.

Focus on my needs and myself.

Spend time with other people.

Spend time with my children.

Have fun with my children.

Parent the way I choose to.

Not feel responsible for fixing others.

Be independent.

Safely leave a relationship I no longer want to be in.

Not engage with individuals or people who are hurtful and/or abusive towards me.

Not live in fear.

DOI: 10.4324/9781003328674-10

3. Pilgrim's amazing people

4. Child's helpers map

5. Additional cut-outs

6.   Pilgrim's body map

7. Child body map

8. Blank house

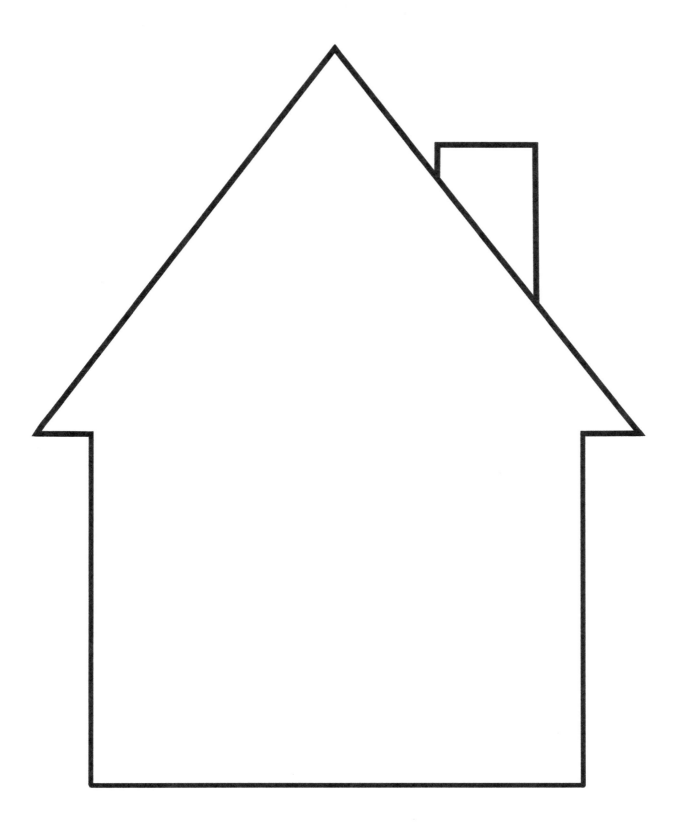

9. Adult's helpers map

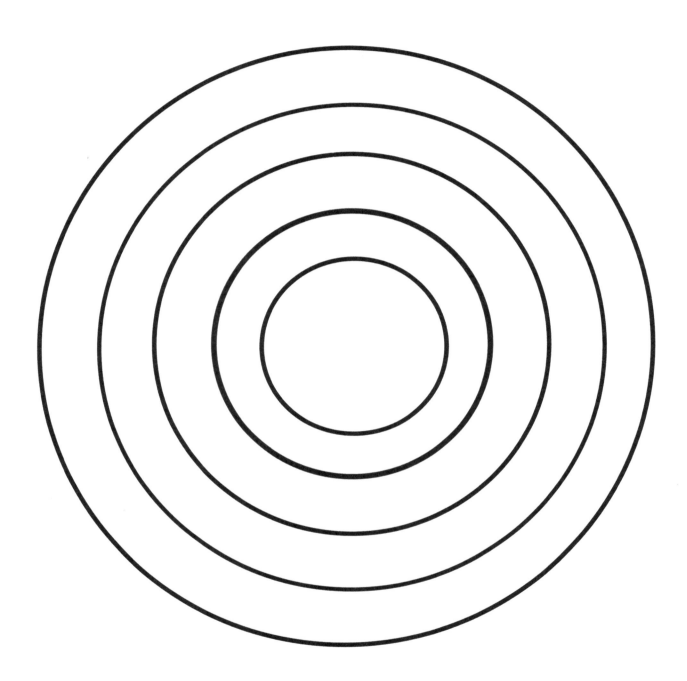

Helplines

Women's Aid is a charity that aims to end domestic violence/abuse against women and children. It provides a wide range of services and runs the national 24 hour 7 days a week confidential domestic abuse helpline.

https://www.womensaid.org.uk/

0808 2000 247

The Survivor's Handbook – Women's Aid (https://www.womensaid.org.uk/information-support/the-survivors -handbook/)

Refuge supports women and children who experience all forms of violence and abuse, including domestic violence, sexual violence, female genital mutilation, forced marriage, so-called honour-based violence and human trafficking and modern slavery. Confidential domestic abuse helpline.

https://www.refuge.org.uk/get-help-now/

0808 2000 247

Men's Advice Line is a charity that offers help and support for male victims of domestic violence. They run a men's helpline.

http://www.mensadviceline.org.uk/

0808 901 0327

Galop run the national lesbian, gay bisexual and trans domestic violence helpline.

www.galop.org.uk

0800 999 5428

Respect has a confidential helpline offering advice, information and support to help individuals to stop being violent and abusive to their partner.

www.respectphoneline.org.uk

0808 802 4040

DOI: 10.4324/9781003328674-12

Rape Crisis is an organisation that offers support and counselling for those affected by rape and sexual abuse.

www.rapecrisis.org.uk

0808 802 9999

National Association for People Abused in Childhood (NAPAC) offers support to adult survivors of all types of childhood abuse, including physical, sexual, emotional abuse or neglect.

https://napac.org.uk/

0808 801 0331

Shelter helps people with housing needs by providing expert advice and support; they also run a national helpline.

https://england.shelter.org.uk

0808 800 4444

NSPCC is the UK's leading children's charity, preventing abuse and helping those affected to recover.

https://www.nspcc.org.uk/

0808 800 5000

Paws Protect is a cat protection fostering service for families fleeing domestic abuse.

www.cats.org.uk/what-we-do/paws-protect

The Dogs Trust the freedom project is a dog pet fostering service for families fleeing domestic abuse.

www.dogstrust.org.uk/help-advice/hope-project-freedom-project/freedom-project

0207 837 0006

RSPCA is the largest animal welfare charity operating in England and Wales. 24-hour cruelty line to report cruelty, neglect or an animal in distress.

https://www.rspca.org.uk/

0300 1234 999

For Babies Sake's vision is to empower parents to break cycles of abuse, transform the life chances of families and move forward with positive change starting with the baby.

www.forbabyssake.org.uk

Domestic Abuse Intervention Program is home to the "Duluth Model", an ever-evolving way of thinking about how a community works together to end domestic violence.

www.theduluthmodel.org

Bright Sky is a safe, easy-to-use app and website that provides practical support and information on how to respond to domestic abuse. It is for anyone experiencing domestic abuse, or who is worried about someone else.

Bright Sky helps you to spot the signs of abuse, know how to respond and help someone find a safe route to support.

Ask for ANI (Action Needed Immediately) is a codeword scheme that enables victims of domestic abuse to discreetly ask for immediate help in participating pharmacies and Jobcentres (Jobs and Benefits Offices in Northern Ireland).

The scheme was developed by the Home Office with the help of partners including the domestic abuse sector, pharmacy associations and the police. It was launched across the UK on 14 January 2021. The scheme is now managed by Hestia's UK Says No More campaign.

Ask for ANI domestic abuse codeword: information for pharmacies – GOV.UK (https://www.gov.uk/guidance /ask-for-ani-domestic-abuse-codeword-information-for-pharmacies)

Hollie Guard is a personal alarm, deterrent, evidence catcher and more. Help protect yourself, a friend or a family member with Hollie Guard.

Silent Solution Guide is a system that you can use if you're in an emergency situation and need police help, but can't speak, Make yourself heard and let the 999 operator know your call is genuine. (https://www .policeconduct.gov.uk/our-work/key-areas-of-work/silent-solution)

References

Beeble, M., Bybee, D., & Sullivan, C. M. (2007) Abusive men's use of children to control their partners and ex-partners. *European Psychologist* 12(1). https://doi.org/10.1027/1016-9040.12.1.54.

Campbell, J., Jones, A. S., Dienemann, J., Kub, J., Schollenberg, J., O'Campo, P., Gielen, A. C., & Wynne, C. (2002) Intimate partner violence and physical health consequences. *Archives of Internal Medicine* 162(10), 1157–1163.

Carpenter, G. L., & Stacks, A. M. (2009) Developmental effects of exposure to intimate partner violence in early childhood: A review of the literature. *Children and Youth Review* 31(8), 831–839. http://doi.org/10.1016/J.childyouth.2009.03.005

Felitti, V., Anda, R., Nordenberg, D., Williamson, D. F., Spitz, A. M., Edwards, V., Koss, M. P., & Marks, J. S. (1998) Relationship of childhood abuse and household dysfunction to many of the leading causes of death in adults. *American Journal of Preventative Medicine* 14(4), 245–258.

Forbes, H., & Post, B. (2009) *Beyond Consequences, Logic and Control: A Love Based Approach to Helping Attachment Challenged Children with Severe Behaviours*. Boulder, CO: Beyond Consequences Institute LLC.

Harne, L. (2011) *Violent Fathers and the Risks to Children: The Need for Change*. Bristol: The Policy Press.

Johnson, M.P (2008). *A Typology of Domestic Violence: Intimate Terrorism, Violent Resistance, and Situational Couple Violence*. Boston, MA: Northeastern University Press.

Katz, E., Nikupeteri, A., & Laitinen, M. (2020) When coercive control continues to harm children: Post-separation fathering, stalking, and domestic violence. *Child Abuse Review* 29(4), 310–324.

Monckton-Smith, J. (2020) *In Control: Dangerous Relationships and How They End in Murder*. London: Bloomsbury.

Pufall, P., & Unsworth, R. (2004) *Rethinking Childhood*. New Brunswick, NJ: Rutgers University Press.

Sheppard, S. K. (2010) Building rapport with children. Sexual Assault Center of Northeast Georgia. www.gacasa.org.

Stark, E. (2007) *Coercive Control: How Men Entrap Women in Personal Life*. New York: Oxford University Press.

Swanson, J., Bowyer, L., & Vetere, A. (2014) Towards a richer understanding of school-age children's experiences of domestic violence: The voices of children and their mothers. *Clinical Child Psychology and Psychiatry* 19(2), 184–201.

Van Der Kolk, B. (2014) *The Body Keeps the Score: Brain, Mind and Body in the Healing of Trauma*. New York: Penguin Books Ltd.

Index